Raising Up Mommy

*Virtues for Difficult
Mothering Moments*

Titles in the Women of Grace® Life Guide Series:

New Age "Healing Hoaxes":
Exposing Reiki, Therapeutic Touch,
and Other New Age Approaches to "Wellness,"
by Johnnette S. Benkovic

Raising a Child in the Heart of the Church:
Advice for Catholic Families
by Johnnette S. Benkovic

Shall We Pray?:
On Christian Meditation and New Age Mysticism
by Johnnette S. Benkovic

Raising Up Mommy:
Virtues for Difficult Mothering Moments
by Heidi Hess Saxton

Addicted to Stuff!:
What to Do When Your Possessions Possess You
by Dale O'Leary

Order online through the Women of Grace® website
(www.womenofgrace.com) or by calling 800-558-5452.

Raising Up Mommy

Virtues for Difficult Mothering Moments

A Women of Grace® Life Guide

Heidi Hess Saxton

Simon Peter Press

For permission to reprint any portion of this book, contact Permissions Editor, Simon Peter Press, Inc. P.O. Box 2187, Oldsmar, FL 34677.

Unless otherwise noted, all Scripture quotations are from the *Revised Standard Version: Catholic Edition*. © 1946, 1952, 1957, 1965, and 1966, by the Division of Christian Education of the National Council of Churches of Christ in the United States of America. Published by Thomas Nelson Publishers for Ignatius Press. All rights reserved.

Excerpts from the English translation of the *Catechism of the Catholic Church* for the United States of America. © 1994, United States Catholic Conference, Inc. – Libreria Editrice Vaticana. English translation of the *Catechism of the Catholic Church, Modifications from the Editio Typica* © 1997, United States Catholic Conference, Inc. – Libreria Editrice Vaticana. All rights reserved.

Nihil Obstat: Msgr. Robert Lunsford, Censor Libororum

Imprimatur: Most Reverend Carl F. Mengeling
Bishop of Lansing, Michigan
February 15, 2007

The Nihil Obstat and Imprimatur are official declarations that a book or pamphlet is free from doctrinal or moral error. No implication is contained therein that those who have granted the Nihil Obstat and Imprimatur agree with the contents, opinions, or statements expressed.

Published by Simon Peter Press, Inc., P.O. Box 2187, Oldsmar, FL 34677
727.417.6639 www.simonpeterpress.com

07 08 09 10 9 8 7 6 5 4 3 2 1

Printed in the United States of America

ISBN: 10: 0-9777430-2-0
ISBN: 13: 978-0-9777430-2-5

LIBRARY OF CONGRESS CATALOGING-IN-PUBLICATION DATA

For valiant Mommies everywhere,
and for my family—who makes the struggle worthwhile.

Table of Contents

CHAPTER ONE:
Who Is This Woman They Call "Mommy"? 1

CHAPTER TWO:
Womanly Virtue –
Heavenly Antidotes with a Feminine Twist 7

CHAPTER THREE:
Pride and Humility – The Feminine Face of Hiddenness 16

CHAPTER FOUR:
Envy and Trust – The Feminine Face of Contentment 24

CHAPTER FIVE:
Gluttony and Temperance –
The Feminine Face of Self-Denial 29

CHAPTER SIX:
Lust and Modesty – The Feminine Face of Intimacy 35

CHAPTER SEVEN:
Anger and Justice – The Feminine Face of Compassion 43

CHAPTER EIGHT:
Greed and Generosity –
The Feminine Face of Hospitality 50

CHAPTER NINE:
Sloth and Prudence – The Feminine Face of Industry 58

CHAPTER TEN:
Raising Up Mommy – A "Pick-Me-Up" Plan 66

CHAPTER ONE

Who Is This Woman
They Call "Mommy"?

*Lay holiness must be worked out in one's ordinary
circumstances, just as is the case with one's lay
apostolate. So, this holiness may be hidden from the
view of most people. But personal holiness is the
indispensable foundation of the Church's mission.
It must be fostered if the rest of the lay apostolate
is to be effective.*

Pope John Paul II,
Christifideles Laici (1.5)

For our first year of foster parenthood, we drove our three kids ninety miles each week into inner-city Detroit to visit their birth parents. One trip was especially memorable. Hopped up on adrenaline, their faces sticky with sugar and hands loaded with gum and Happy Meal trinkets, the kids were barely strapped into their car seats before the bickering started.

"M-O-M! Christopher's touching me!" yelled Cheyenne, five.

"No!" Christopher retorted. It was his favorite (and often only) word.

"Yi-yi-yi-yi-YAK!" burbled nine-month-old Sarah.

"M-O-M! Sarah puked," they yelled together. It was the first time that afternoon they had agreed about anything.

That did it. The agency waiting room had been a zoo, and I hadn't been able to study for my mid-term that afternoon. I was still working part-time and going to school part-time, trying to finish up my master's degree for the not-too-distant future when

Craig retired and I became the primary breadwinner. Staying home with the children full-time was not something we could afford to do, even if I wanted to.

The fact was, I didn't want to. Three months at home alone with the children had convinced me that—whatever my other gifts might be —I was not a "natural mother." Sure, I could sing a million little ditties, and play "How Big is Baby" with the best of them. But when it came to the motherly virtues: patience and kindness and self-control, I was perpetually about a quart short. Especially when I was sleep deprived, which was constantly. After three months, the kids were still waking at all hours of the day and night—and never at the same time. *There is a reason God gives babies to twenty-year-olds*, I decided. Something had to give.

The first thing to go was my serenity. "Mommy Monster" manifested itself the first time on the ride home from the agency that day, surprising all of us. My outburst shut them up for a full thirty seconds, eyes wide with wonder. Even the baby stopped her "baby cussing" long enough to watch mom get red in the face and hop up and down. Finally I heard a shaky whisper from the back seat: *"Mommy monster …"*

That night, ashamed of my behavior, I turned on my computer and sent out a virtual SOS to every mother I knew well enough to ask this pressing question: How do you tame *your* Mommy Monster? What do you do when you've had it up to *here* and they won't let you implode in peace?

Cyberspace was filled with empathetic chuckles. Good Samaritans sent books and tapes, including my favorite, Julie Barnhill's *She's Gonna Blow!* Learn to recognize the signals, the author suggested: clenched fists, overreacting to small annoyances, and headaches. Then find ways to de-stress and regain perspective.

"Give yourself a time-out with God," another friend

suggested. This sounded great, though I wasn't sure how to manage this with a three-year-old clutching my thigh and a nine-month-old strapped to my front. But I began to take little steps— a verse taped over the kitchen sink, a tape of Taize music in the shower, taking a deep breath and lifting my hands in offering (rather than beating my pillow in frustration) upon being awakened for the fourth time in as many hours.

While this helped, I knew this would not completely take care of the problem. I had been raised by a stay-at-home mom who, despite her many gifts, also struggled to maintain equilibrium in the face of external pressures and internal limitations. I did not want my kids to live in the shadow of rages and mood swings. For their sake, I needed to find a release valve.

❧ Action Step: Find Your "Release Valve" ✐

How does stress affect you—headaches, mood swings, other aches and pains? This week, be mindful of initial stress symptoms that indicate you need to de-stress. Create a list of simple things you can do to help yourself, keeping in mind the need to balance the needs of both body and soul. A few things to remember:

☙ Prevention is often the best cure. Get up ten minutes earlier than the rest of your family to sip a cup of herbal tea and spend a few minutes with God.

☙ Take full advantage of the sacraments, particularly daily Mass and reconciliation as often as you need it. The graces are there for the taking, and you need all the reinforcements you can get during this harried time of life!

☙ Take a vigorous walk or exercise while listening to Christian music.

❦ Remember that kids are often orneriest when they need love most. If they are driving you crazy, get down on the floor for a (gentle) tickle or pillow fight!

❦ Get in the car, turn on the radio, and sing along loudly— in a different key!

❦ Tape your favorite psalm strategically to the bathroom wall, for the next time you need a "Mommy time out" in a hurry.

❦ Call your mother ... No, not the one you reach by phone. Send up a little heavenly S.O.S. "Mary, pray for me. I doubt YOUR little angel ever flushed a washcloth down the toilet, but MY little angel is driving me to distraction!"

❦ Don't forget to breathe... If it will help, grab an onion and start chopping, so you can cry a little, too. (The onion is a cover, so you don't freak out the kids.)

Spotting Your Mommy Monster

Now, some women reading this will chuckle with a faint sense of relief and start to put down this booklet, saying, "Wow. She really is a nut ... thank God I don't have a Mommy Monster at MY house!"

Wait! Don't close the book just yet. Just as no two women are alike, our weaknesses find expression in very different ways. One woman may be a yeller ... another resorts to secret stashes of Mallowmars or Mike's Hard Lemonade. Still another will pull inward, closing herself off from her husband and his needs; others will ignore their own needs, working themselves into an early martyr's grave. A select few look down their noses at other women who cannot keep it together as they can.

Thank God, this last tendency is not a great temptation for most mothers. In His wisdom, God orchestrates the events of motherhood (or so it seems) to cultivate a bumper crop of humility in most of us. And so, I am writing this to you not as a woman who has perfected the art of mothering, or one who has arrived near the pinnacle of sainthood. Ask my husband—I have a long way to go. However, I have had the opportunity to study from the "best of the blessed," and have noticed practical streams of thought that can shore our defenses against the darts the enemy uses to assault homes and families. I offer some of those thoughts here, in hopes that they will encourage you to take a closer look at these favorite tricks of the evil one—and how you can better stand on guard against them.

In this book, we will be exploring each of what the Church Fathers considered the seven "deadly sins," particularly as they pertain to the womanly vocations, and consider the spiritual "antidote" for each one. We will also consider seven quintessentially feminine "faces" of these virtues, and show how our distinctively feminine gifts enable us to cultivate these virtues not only in our own lives, but within our homes as well.

As God leads us into battle against these monsters, let's begin with a psalm of praise!

> Gracious is the Lord and just;
> > Yes, our Lord is merciful.
> The Lord keeps the little ones;
> > I was brought low, and he saved me.
> Return, O my soul, to your tranquility,
> > For the Lord has been good to you.
> For he has freed my soul from death,
> > My eyes from tears, my feet from stumbling.
> I shall walk before the Lord
> > In the lands of the living.
> > > Psalm 116:5–9

For Reflection and Discussion

❦ Close your eyes, and ask God to bring to your mind someone who is struggling to be a good parent today. Write that person a note to let her know you are thinking of her—or better yet, make a "play date"!

❦ "Eek! I'm becoming my mother!" Have you noticed any personal weaknesses (or strengths) that you swore you would never foist upon your children … and yet, you find yourself doing just that? Are any of these an expression of a deadly vice? If so … how are you going to "break the cycle"?

Write your answers to these questions in your Study Guide.

CHAPTER TWO

Womanly Virtue:
Heavenly Antidotes with a Feminine Twist

In Mary, women find the secret of their
femininity and dignity.
"In the light of Mary, the Church sees
in the face of women the reflection of a beauty
which mirrors the loftiest sentiments
of which the human heart is capable:
the self-offering totality of love;
the strength that is capable of bearing the greatest sorrows;
limitless fidelity and tireless devotion to work;
the ability to combine penetrating intuition with words
of support and encouragement."

Pope John Paul II,
Redemptoris Mater (101)

When I first met Meghan, I thought she was the perfect parent. *Her* six children always remembered to say please and thank you, shook hands with strangers at the sign of peace, and sat through every homily with the same rapt attention that my border collie exhibits when you wave a choice bit of steak under her nose. Plus, Meghan home-schooled; she *wanted* to be around her children 24/7!

The Perry family always arrived at Mass well before the bell tolled, smiling and serene (or so I heard ... For the first three months we were lucky to slide into our pew by the opening hymn, and within minutes I was usually tempted to put at least one of them in the offering basket.)

Of course, the truth is always a little different from the outside, and time changes things. Meghan has since been blessed with another child whose deportment initially bore a far stronger resemblance to the Exorcist Baby than that of her other little angels. "He's a little fussier than the other ones were," she admits. I confess I find it much easier to like her now, and together we laugh about my initial (inferiority- producing) impressions.

I still admire her, too—perhaps even more than I did previously. Her smiling serenity is now laced with a warmth and compassion that inspires me to follow her lead. I want to know how she manages, with seven kids (including a new baby), to keep the floors clear enough to move from one room to the next without stepping on a Veggie Tale.

This influential path of womanly virtue is not an idea that originated with me. St. Teresa of Avila taught her sisters that the best way to correct a fault (in ourselves or in others) is to practice the corresponding virtue. When the early Church Fathers identified seven deadly sins, others prescribed the antidote: The corresponding virtue that would lessen—and ultimately break—the grip of the deadly vice.

Most of us can rattle off at least a few of the "Deadly Seven": pride, envy, gluttony, greed, lust, anger, sloth. We find it much harder to identify any of these "big" faults in ourselves at times; however, within the vocation of motherhood these deadly vices can insinuate themselves in ways that may surprise us.

For example, the sin of **pride** (overconfidence in self) can masquerade as selflessness, often with an air of martyred resentment. "No one can do this like I can … I'd better do it myself!" As mothers, we must guard against this temptation of false self-sufficiency and perfectionism, and learn to lighten up. How? By practicing a corresponding virtue: **faith** (having confidence in God, and extending that confidence to our children). **Humility** is also handy for pride-bug bites, holding our tongues when the impulse strikes to disassociate from any efforts that are less than perfect—or that surpass our own. "Yes, dear, I agree. These biscuits *are* the best ... Martha made them!"

The opposite of **envy** (disordered desire for another's goods) is **hope** (trust in God's providential will). As mothers, we can quickly grow discontented with our families and ourselves if we fall into the trap of comparing ourselves with the way others *appear to be.* "Oh, I could never be as organized as she is..." "Her kids are always so well behaved." Instead, we trust in God, that He has given us everything we need to accomplish His will for our lives.

The opposite of **gluttony** (disordered desire to consume) is **temperance** (detachment from physical goods in favor of spiritual ones). Traditionally, this applies to food and drink—and as a nation of overweight people, this is certainly something to consider. However, as mothers we must guard against inordinate consumption of all kinds: the media, parenting books, alcohol, chocolate... If you find yourself becoming dependent, or spending too much time, on something, why not "fast" from it for a while?

The opposite of **lust** (disordered desire for sensory pleasure) is **courage** (oriented toward God's pleasure and our lasting rewards). "If it feels good, just do it"—following this cultural credo will get us in hot water every time. As mothers, we must zealously guard against these and other messages that tear at the fabric of family life.

The opposite of **anger** (inordinate sensitivity to personal justice) is **justice** (oriented to what is good for and in others). Feelings of anger can indicate a spiritual "infection" from a wound that has never healed. When you feel anger rise, ask God to show you the root cause. What does He want you to learn from it?

The opposite of **sloth** (inordinate desire for leisure and convenience) is **prudence** (which leads to wisdom). Is the clutter in your home closing in on you? Do you have the local take-out on speed dial? Do you avoid getting more active in church because you are already "too busy"? Ask God to show you where your priorities should be — where you can cut back. Then ask your husband what he thinks! The answers may surprise you.

The opposite of **greed** (inordinate attachment to physical goods) is **generosity** (love expressed in self-denial). In motherhood, the temptation to greed may take on distinctive forms: Are there any areas of your life where your "security" is something other than God? Do you hold your children loosely, willing to offer them back to God in service if He calls them? Are you content to live within your means— financial, material, and vocational?

With this in mind, what virtue should you put into practice this week? Ask God to make you especially sensitive to opportunities to practice virtue. Write down your experiences— which were easy for you, and which were more difficult? Once you have identified spiritual "flab," pray for strength and "exercise opportunities" to overcome it!

✒ Action Step: Gear Up for Spiritual "Wait Training" ✎

In her article "Wait Training for Advent" (*Canticle*, November 2006), Woodeene Koenig-Bricker points out the similarities between physical and spiritual weight training, showing how we can incorporate principles of weight training in the cultivation of virtue.

> *You don't use the same types of weights or exercises to increase endurance as you do to pump up muscle. If you want stamina, you use lighter weights, but lift them many times. If you want strength, you lift heavier weights fewer times.*
>
> *Remember that you can't accomplish both at the same*

time. Someone who is bodybuilding can't simultaneously be training for a marathon. You must choose which one you want right now. There will be time later to develop the other spiritual muscles.

So ... As you read the chapters that follow, ask yourself: Does this particular weakness hit in short spurts, intermittently, requiring simple endurance so as not to let it gain on you? Or do you battle with a particular vice frequently, necessitating the cultivation of strong virtue?

Someone who suffers from periodic bouts of greed, for example, might decide to volunteer at a soup kitchen once a month (a great corporal work of mercy for the whole family!). Someone who cannot pass a mall without maxing out her credit cards, on the other hand, may need a full-blown "spending fast" (holding herself accountable to her husband or a spiritual advisor) in order to get her "monster" under control.

The Incarnation Principle

Most of us have a nondescript memento or two that forever connects us with an important part of our past: old letters and faded photographs, a dilapidated childhood toy, or a class ring. For me, it's an old tobacco pouch that belonged to my father. He hasn't smoked in years, but one whiff of the leather pouch and its tobacco remnants, and I am transported to childhood, stirring the soup as Dad reads his paper at the kitchen table.

When God created the first man and woman in His image, He created us not just as spiritual beings (like the angels) or physical beings (like the animals); we are body-soul composites. As a result, we relate to the spiritual world through the physical one, unlocking reason and memory through our senses.

In the Old Testament, God spoke to Moses through the

burning bush, and to Pharaoh through the ten plagues. In the New Testament, God speaks most forcefully through the Incarnation, then again and again through the miracles of Christ and His apostles.

This "Incarnation Principle"—that God initiates contact with humans through the physical world—is at the heart of the Catholic worldview. As Catholic women, this is a double-edged sword. We can get ourselves into all sorts of trouble if we lose that essential corporal-spiritual connection by focusing too much on one or the other: Turning Advent into one long sensory "race to the manger" by packing every moment with planning and preparations, robs us of the spiritual insights of the season.

Equally depressing is any attempt to "sterilize" the physical reality of the Incarnation in a misguided effort to enter into the holiness of the moment. The glittering lights, fragrant pine boughs, immaculate crèche scene and gently wafting organ music can draw us back to that first Christmas: the scratchy straw, wailing Infant, and smelly sheep. It was no Norman Rockwell moment, to be sure. But in the harsh reality of the Incarnation, God made His most ardent declaration of love for the human race. This same passion that first induced Him to lie squirming in a feeding trough, entices Him to come to us again and again in the Eucharist, under the appearance of bread and wine.

By embracing wholeheartedly the provisions He made for us before returning to heavenly glory, we become most fully the human persons God created us to be. In the sacraments, we receive Him uniquely and completely; in the Church, we are safe in the bosom of His Family. Above all, to love the Savior is to love His mother, who gave Him all that made Him truly human.

Heavenly Virtues, Expressed in Womanly Terms

By imitating the Blessed Mother, women have unique opportunities to embody the great spiritual virtues, passing them through the filter of our femininity. As we read in the Catechism (2516):

> Because man is a *composite being, spirit and body,* there already exists a certain tension in him; a certain struggle of tendencies between 'spirit' and 'flesh' develops. But in fact this struggle belongs to the heritage of sin. It is a consequence of sin and at the same time a confirmation of it. It is part of the daily experience of the spiritual battle:
>
> For the Apostle, it is not a matter of despising and condemning the body which with the spiritual soul constitutes man's nature and personal subjectivity. Rather, he is concerned with the morally *good or bad* works, or better, the permanent dispositions—virtues and vices—which are the fruit of *submission* (in the first case) or of *resistance* (in the second case) to *the saving action of the Holy Spirit.* For this reason the Apostle writes: 'If we live by the Spirit, let us also walk by the Spirit'" (John Paul II, *DeV* 55; cf. *Gal* 5:25).

Through our particular gifts—our intuition, relatedness, and life-nurturing abilities—God entrusts to us the task of sweetening the anti-venom of deadly sin. Just as the vices have a particular expression in the feminine person, so do the virtues.

Therefore, God counteracts the deadly sin of lust not only with the virtues of courage and modesty, but with the feminine gift of relational intimacy. He restores the balance of a soul caught in greed not only with the charitable impulses of generosity, but through the distinctively feminine gift of hospitality. (This is not to say that men are incapable of intimacy and hospitality, only that in His wisdom God delegated to the feminine soul the ability to wield these gifts with supernatural precision and grace.)

In the chapters that follow, we will explore each vice in turn, and see how God has not only charged us with the task of neutralizing their effects in our lives, but given us the ability to use those weaknesses and failings to strengthen ourselves and our families, that we might grow in true spiritual perfection. In this guide, we will examine each of the vices and virtues in turn, and reflect upon the graces God has provided for us to emerge victorious. As His Word promises us:

"No temptation has overtaken you that is not common to man. God is faithful, and he will not let you be tempted beyond your strength, but with the temptation will also provide the way of escape, that you may be able to endure it."

1 Corinthians 10:13

For Reflection and Discussion

❧ One of the most well-known and often-quoted passages of St. Teresa's writing is this prayer of trust. In what one area do you need to apply it to your life today?

> *Let nothing trouble you, let nothing frighten you*
> *All things pass away, but God never changes.*
> *Patience obtains all things, for she who possesses God*
> *Wants for nothing… God alone suffices.*
> Teresa of Avila

❧ How do we as mothers "incarnate" Christ to our children, even in our moments of weakness?

❧ Based on what you know of the seven deadly vices so far, which do you struggle with most and why? Write down your thoughts and come back to them at the end of the study, to see whether you view it differently.

Write your answers to these questions in your Study Guide.

CHAPTER THREE

The Feminine Face of Hiddenness

Parent Trap #1: Pride
Virtuous Antidote: Humility

Pride will bring me low,
but the lowly in spirit will obtain honor.
Proverbs 29:23

Before my husband and I became parents—overnight—to two-year-old Christopher and six-month-old Sarah (along with their older sister, who was later adopted by another couple), I had not a clue how difficult it would be to dive into the deep end of the parenting pool. Before I had children, for example, I assumed training a toddler to sit through Mass would be a snap.

The kids had been with us about a week when we took them to church for the first time. I was scheduled to cantor at the piano that week, so Sarah spent most of her time dozing on Craig's shoulder. Christopher, clearly out of his element, clutched my thigh and howled. He didn't understand what I was doing, but one thing was for sure: He had lost one foster mother already that week, and he was not going to lose sight of me without a fight.

The following week we tried another, more "child friendly" parish. Christopher was still refusing to come within arm's reach of my husband, the gentle giant. So it should not have surprised us when Father Will reached out his hand to bless our son, and Christopher responded with an emphatic "NO!" and a surprisingly accurate left hook.

"Brat," I heard someone behind us mutter as we beat a hasty retreat to our pew. Fortunately Father Will has a good sense of humor, which he got to exercise again seven days later when Christopher bid the priest good-bye by grabbing his vestments six inches south of the equator, the highest place his two-year-old hands could reach.

This was new territory for me. All my life, I had been on the "giving" end of Church life—serving in some capacity or other, often in conspicuous places such as cantoring or leading the choir. Of course, I felt pretty conspicuous in this situation, too—but it wasn't a good feeling. Frankly, most weeks I went away feeling as though I was not the only one there who wished we had all just stayed home.

What Is "Motherly" Pride?

The haughty face of pride takes many guises in the life of a wife and mother.

For some, it is the "martyr" complex, a woman who is so convinced that no one could do _____ as thoroughly /efficiently/creatively/cheaply as she, she works herself into a hole. At first glance, she may seem like the "perfect" mother and wife in that she waits on her family hand and foot—but it is service with a chain. By refusing to teach her children to participate in the upkeep of the family, she is keeping them unnecessarily dependent on her.

Other women struggle with "Busy Bee" tendencies, finding it impossible to imagine that God might have someone else in mind for a certain task that catches our attention (if indeed it is still necessary for that something to be done). I wrestle with this one at times myself. Some time ago I noticed a certain announcement in the bulletin, calling for the fourth time for someone to fill in a needed spot on a church committee. I pointed it out to Craig, wondering idly if I should just do it. My mild-mannered husband sputtered, "Are you *kidding* me?" He was right. My Bible-teaching, hymn-singing, missions-minded "public self" was being tempted to overextend (again) in well-intended but ultimately misguided service.

Our children had been with us for about a year when the bulletin announced the need for lectors to serve at the six weekend Masses. Thanks to my seminary studies, I had ample training for the task—and yet, my daughter was not pleased the first time I went to take my place at the lectern. She raised such a fuss, in fact, ("Nooo, Mommy! Don't go up there! That's for *Father Will!*") that Craig had to carry her out.

This was embarrassing, and my first instinct was to back out of serving in this capacity, reasoning that my first responsibility was to teach my children to participate at Mass with a measure of decorum. Craig wasn't sure, and finally I called our pastoral associate for her advice.

As always, Ceci was kind yet direct. "Heidi," she explained patiently, "Each person has a job to do in order for the parish to run smoothly. Can you think of a better way to educate your daughter about this fact? You have the training, and the ability. She needs to see you serving God, too."

And so I continued to take my turn in the lector rotation. And Ceci was right—very soon Sarah began to ask me each week if it was my turn to read.

Then, a few weeks ago, the lesson came full circle as I slipped out of my seat and approached the lectern to do the first reading … and felt a little hand grab onto mine. Sarah had decided that *she* was going to help, too. And although I was well aware of the risk inherent with exposing a four-year-old to an audience, I squeezed her little mitt and toted her along. To my eternal relief, she stood there, wide-eyed and still as a bit of statuary, listening to the story in 2 Kings about the multiplication of the loaves.

When we stand before God one day, we will have to account for what we did with all the time, treasure, and lives He entrusted to our care. And yet, God is most concerned about our fidelity to the "inner circle" of our vocation. After corralling my two preschoolers through a typical Sunday, I have a fresh appreciation for what Jesus meant when he told his disciples, "*Suffer* the little children to come unto me..." Devotion, like holiness, is not passed through the bloodstream, but caught gradually, over time.

Oh, sure, I've read those "How to silence your children in three Masses or less" articles, but I've never believed them. God designed the family as the means by which each of its members is sanctified, a process measured in years, not weeks. If Jesus is our ticket to heaven, our children are like the malaria shots: They prepare us for the trip and keep us healthy on the road—even though it might require a bit of short-term discomfort.

Do You Struggle With Pride?

> "*Take care not to frighten away by stern rigor poor sinners who are trying to lay bare the shocking state of their souls. Speak to them rather of the great mercy of God... sometimes people are helped by your telling them of your own lamentable past.*"
>
> St. Francis Xavier
> Quotable Saints, by Ronda Chervin

Pride is inordinate self-love, caring more about another's opinion (even our own) than what God thinks. It is at the root of all hypocrisy, prejudice, and presumption.

Do you wrestle with this particular deadly sin? Take this little self-test, basing your answers on your most *typical* behavior, based on the preponderance of evidence. (Hint: How do you think a person who knows you well would answer on your behalf?)

Responding positively to several of these questions may indicate you are in need of a "lift" of virtue; consider whether it is strength or endurance that you need.

True or false ...

T/F Although Scriptures tell us to give so that "your right hand doesn't know what your left is doing," I'm disappointed if word doesn't leak out about my good deed, at least among those close to me.

T/F I have a hard time letting anyone but me run a program or activity with which I am associated. Controlling the outcome is important to me.

T/F It bothers me to hear someone else complimented or get credit for something in which I was more heavily involved.

T/F My expectations—both of myself and of other people— keep people from getting close to me.

T/F It is easier for me to rationalize than to apologize, and to assign blame than accept it.

T/F I have lost friendships due to an entrenched misunderstanding or grudge.

T/F It is difficult for me to learn from "ordinary" people— especially those whose perspective is very different (e.g. less educated or affluent, or from a different religious or cultural background from my own).

T/F If there is a "preferred" section in heaven, I secretly believe that I have a reserved seat.

T/F When bad things happen to other people, I tell myself God would never let something like that happen to ME.

T/F Though I'd never admit it out loud, I sometimes suspect God loves me more than He loves some other people.

❧ Action Steps: Defeating Motherly Pride ❧

Do you need endurance or strength in order to overcome this particular weakness in your own life? Consider one or more of the following.

☙ *For endurance:* Write a note to someone you find hard to love, letting her know that she is on your mind, and that you have been praying for her this week. (Don't mention the reason you chose her in particular.) Put the note on your prayer shelf, where you will remember to pray for that person daily for a whole week. Then mail the note.

☙ *For strength:* Select a task that you've been putting off or avoiding because there are others who could do it better or more efficiently than you. This could be a volunteer assignment at church, or a chore your husband hasn't gotten around to. Then do it! (Extra points if you manage to pull it off without anyone noticing or thanking you.)

Hiddenness: The Feminine Face of *Humility*

You'd think the sight of a talking snake would have silenced Eve long enough for reason to kick in. Instead, she stuck her neck out … and then she stuck her hand out to take the fruit, tantalized by the idea that she might have perfect knowledge, like God. Her husband could not stop her, her conscience did not stop her—she rushed ahead, without thought for the consequences.

The New Eve was no less courageous, and yet she had a quality our first mother did not possess: Alone in her room, she gave humble assent to God's plan, sent by the angel. Then she rushed off to give her cousin Elizabeth the news: She, too, was to be a mother. She was unmarried, and no doubt her pregnancy caused those close to her moments of consternation. And yet, by her hidden obedience, she liberated all mankind—just as the first woman had put them all in captivity.

For many women, motherhood is the means by which our basest desires are purified. Every selfish, proud, and vain impulse is worn away (at times literally); even desires that were appropriate for a time must be set aside in order for the woman to pass through the crucible of motherhood.

As a single adult, I had a great job, lots of friends, and a schedule that was mine alone to keep. There were challenges as well—it could be lonely at times. On the other hand, I could pretty much do as I pleased, and if someone was a cause of consternation or aggravation, I could minimize the contact I had with him or her.

As a mom, my life is no longer my own. Not only am I responsible for my own spiritual development, God wants me to help three others along to heaven—primarily by the power of my own example. Talk about living in a fishbowl! Instead of writing beautiful stories (or editing the delightful prose of other writers), I find myself pushed into a daily grind of dirty floors, dirtier faces, and endless choruses of, "MOOOM! I'm HUNGRY!"

And this, my friend, is the life of hiddenness. Of detachment. Of relinquishment. Of humility. And between you and me, this particular path of virtue is not an easy climb. It is the way of the cross, the way of self-donation.

This is not to say you won't sometimes be in the public eye. There are many women with the gift of teaching, of encouragement, and even of prophecy. You may well find yourself standing up in church, reading from the lectionary.

But be prepared: The eyes who are watching you most intently
—and the ones that matter most—are the little eyes who will be
sitting beside you tonight at another important reading. *Velveteen
Rabbit,* anyone?

For Reflection and Discussion

෮ Is there an area of my life that I am particularly prone
to fall into the temptation of pride? If so, how can I
cultivate humility in this area?

෮ Can I think of a recent experience that was painful at
the time, but that I now see was God's way of showing
me that I was relying more in my own inner resources
than on Him? If I were to face this again, how would I
handle the situation differently?

෮ Is there someone from who I am currently estranged
because of a lack of humility? How can I begin to mend
this breach—regardless of who was most at fault?

Write your answers to these questions in your Study Guide.

CHAPTER FOUR

The Feminine Face of Contentment

Parent Trap #2: Envy
Virtuous Antidote: Trust

I will not pass by the truth;
neither will I travel in the company of sickly envy,
for envy does not associate with wisdom.
Wisdom 6:22–23

Almost every girl dreams of the day her Prince Charming will get down on one knee and slip a sparkling, appropriately weighty gemstone on her third finger. (Marilyn Monroe insisted that diamonds are a "girl's best friend"; I held out for the guy who understood me well enough to proffer a sapphire.)

Sometime after that "I do" soars heavenward, however, a subtle transformation happens. It caught me by surprise, actually. I had always been a bit of a wanderer, relying on no one but myself and sure that I would continue drawing a paycheck long after the dust had settled on our new china. In reality, no sooner had that wedding ring slipped on my finger, I developed an indescribable urge to stay home.

While the transition affects other couples very differently, most experience a time of adjustment … even disillusionment. "If I had known this was what I was signing up for, I might have had second thoughts." At this point, the couple has a choice: to hold on tighter, to "cleave" with greater intentionality and confidence—or to start turning inward, ultimately becoming more like roommates than soul mates.

Envy, then, becomes the mortar that turns bricks of anger and disillusionment, of betrayal and hurt, into a wall of superficiality and politeness, affections that make the blood run cold and the heart wander. Envy that deadens the soul long before breath leaves the body.

Do You Struggle With Envy?

Envy is an inordinate desire to possess another's gifts, to the point that one comes to disregard or even deny one's own. Because of envy, we lose the ability to trust, and sacrificing the intimacy of relationship in the process.

Do you wrestle with this particular deadly sin? Take this little self-test, basing your answers on your most *typical* behavior, based on the preponderance of evidence. Responding positively to several of these questions may indicate you are in need of a "lift" of virtue; consider whether it is strength or endurance that you need.

True or false …

T/F If I had known what marriage would be like, I might have stayed single.

T/F I want to be _____ (a wife, a mother, a widow, financially successful, etc.) so much, it is hard for me to be around friends who have attained that milestone.

T/F I get a knot in the pit of my stomach whenever I write our Christmas letter; our lives aren't as interesting as other families'.

T/F I never invite church friends over because I'm afraid of what they'll think of the house—some of them are doctors' wives, after all.

T/F My parents love my sibling(s) more than me; I have story after story to prove it.

T/F I spend a day baking the perfect cupcakes for the school bake sale, only to feel like a failure when someone else brings in three cheesecakes.

T/F I never pray out loud in our mother's group because I'll become tongue-tied or forget what I'm saying—others in the group do it so much better!

T/F When I hear of other kids getting special treatment, I am quick to fight for my child(ren)'s rights.

T/F When I watch certain programs on T.V., I find myself becoming discontent with my own home and family.

T/F My family's life would be happier if my husband were more like my friends' husbands, and I'd be much happier if I could be more like _____.

With hope and trust, we must continually offer every aspect of our family life—past, present, and future—back to God, knowing that God loves our children even more than we do. While we want to provide everything our children need, we must continue to remain aware that it is ultimately God who provides for us all.

✎ Action Steps: Defeating Motherly Envy ✐

Do you need endurance or strength in order to overcome this particular weakness in your own life? Consider one or more of the following.

❦ *For endurance:* This week during your prayer time, create a list of 100 things for which you are thankful. These might range from the general (for the beauty of autumn leaves) to the personally relevant (for so-and-so, the perfectly coiffed doctor's wife who usually bugs me, who prayed for me at our last women's meeting). Then each day for a month, read over your list during your prayer time.

❦ *For strength:* Does the same issue cause you to become angry or resentful each time you think of it? Pray for supernatural grace to release its power in your life. Write a letter detailing all the particulars of the situation, then burn it up or bury it in your backyard. Each time you are tempted to become resentful, light the candle or shovel another spoonful of dirt on the mound. Then go to confession.

Contentment: The Feminine Face of Trust

Teresa of Avila (d.1582) taught her sisters, "There are two virtues most necessary to the spiritual life in addition to love. The first is detachment, and the other is humility." This holy detachment is at the heart of true contentment. That is not to say that we should simply accept everything that comes our way, as St. Teresa herself demonstrated.

At a time when a woman's choices were limited to marriage or the convent, this holy woman nearly single-handedly reformed the laxities of the Carmelite order of her day, and in her lifetime established thirty-two monasteries, including sixteen convents for her sisters, the Discalced (shoeless) Carmelites.

However, the way of contentment that St. Paul characterized in his epistle to the Philippians (4:11–13) provides a unique image of what we as women must strive to attain within our own hearts: "I have learned, in whatever state I am, to be content. I know how to be abased, and I know how to abound; in any and all circumstances I have learned the secret of facing plenty and hunger, abundance and want. I can do all things in him who strengthens me."

In many ways, motherhood is one long goodbye. Goodbye to privacy and to self-absorption. Goodbye to extra cash and to spare time. Ultimately, we say goodbye even to daily mothering, content to work ourselves out of a job … the ultimate detachment this side of death. Our children will not always share our dreams, ideals, and expectations for their future. And yet, this too is a matter of trust: Ultimately, it is not our will, but God's, that they must follow.

For Reflection and Discussion

❦ Can I think of a time when my admiration of someone else's gift induced me to put myself down? What would have been a better response?

❦ Do I have one or more gifts that I have neglected because there was someone else who was more gifted than me? Will I have to explain to the Master one day why I "hid my talents" when He returns? (See Matthew 25:14–30.)

❦ Am I a contented person? Is there an area of my life about which I am dissatisfied, and about which I need to change my attitude? Reminder: the Sacrament of Reconciliation is a good place to start.

Write your answers to these questions in your Study Guide.

CHAPTER FIVE

The Feminine Face of Self-Denial

Parent Trap #3: Gluttony
Virtuous Antidote: Temperance

... the Son of man came eating and drinking,
and they say, 'Behold, a glutton and a drunkard,
a friend of tax collectors and sinners!'
Yet wisdom is justified by her deeds.
Matthew 11:19

Eating can be about much more than merely providing nutrients to the body. For many of us, it is also an affirmation of what it is to be human, celebrating with all the senses the reality of the physical world.   The brilliant colors of the pomegranate and kiwi, the scent and sizzle of roasting onions on the Sunday roast, the sweet explosion of corn and watermelon on the hottest days of summer, and the chewy crust of a freshly baked loaf of sourdough are all a cause to revel in the goodness of the One who made us.

Nothing in the Gospels suggests that Jesus and His apostles avoided these sensory pleasures. The Pharisees denounced Jesus for His association with "tax collectors and sinners" (Luke 7:34), and the Lord performed His very first public miracle by turning water into wine at a wedding feast (John 2).

A problem arises, however, when the pursuit of these pleasures becomes an end in itself. The glutton is one who has lost sight of the Source of these gifts as well as the God-given call to faithful stewardship, ensuring the equitable distribution of these gifts to all who need them.

Do You Struggle with Gluttony?

"Do we take as much care of our soul as of our body? O my children! let us no longer live for the pleasure of eating; let us live as the saints have done; let us mortify ourselves as they were mortified. The saints never indulged themselves in the pleasures of good cheer. Their pleasure was to feed on Jesus Christ! Let us follow their footsteps on this earth, and we shall gain the crown which they have in Heaven."

St. John Vianney

The glutton is one whose quest for sensory pleasure, particularly with regard to food, turns a necessary good into something physically and spiritually unhealthful, feeding the carnal passions and deadening the soul to the cries of the needy. As mothers, our own habits—conscious or otherwise—find their mark in our children, who learn far more from our actions than our words.

Unlike the Gnostics, who believed the physical realm to be evil, the Catholic recognizes the good of all God's gifts—while resisting any tendency to form inordinate attachments to them, lest they rob us of a higher, spiritual good.

Do you struggle with gluttony? Take this little self-test, basing your answers on your most *typical* behavior, based on the preponderance of evidence. Responding positively to several of these questions may indicate you are in need of a "lift" of virtue; consider whether it is strength or endurance that you need.

True or false ...

T/F When I am feeling anxious, frustrated, or depressed, I rely on certain "comfort foods" (such as alcohol or chocolate) to help me feel better.

T/F It would be a real hardship if I had to give up _____ for Lent, or for health reasons.

T/F I tend to make the same recipes over and over, motivated by what my kids like rather than cultivating healthy eating habits.

T/F The women in my family have always shown their love with food; my most powerful memories are associated with food.

T/F When my kids are bored, they always ask for a snack.

T/F I have lied about my eating or drinking habits to avoid embarrassment.

T/F Money is tight, so I rarely make meals for other families having hard times—or I spend as little as possible, to be sure my own family is not deprived.

T/F I hoard my favorite snacks, and send only what I don't like or can't use to the food bank at church.

T/F During Lent we usually wind up "cheating" a little— especially when we eat with non-Catholics.

T/F I cheat on my diet so often that I don't admit it in confession ... I know I'll just do it again!

❦ Action Steps: Defeating Mother Gluttony ✑

Do you need endurance or strength in order to overcome this particular weakness in your own life? Consider one or more of the following.

❦ *For endurance:* Select one healthful habit you would like your family to acquire. Create a chart and post it in your kitchen, having your family check it off each day. The one who is most diligent wins a prize (no dishes for a week!).

❦ *For strength:* What homemade treat or other delicacy do you find impossible to pass up? At your next opportunity, spend a day making a large batch – and bring every last crumb to the local retirement home, soup kitchen, or group home. No fair "taste testing"!

Self-Denial: The Feminine Face of Moderation

Truth be told, this chapter is difficult for me to write, primarily because I have the strong sense that I have not yet acquired this particular virtue to the degree I need to. Physically, the signs are apparent—I am as heavy as I've ever been in my life. My stamina is low and I frequently find myself coping with a whole litany of aches and pains—from migraines to foot cramps—that (let's face it) makes it difficult to keep up with the demands of a young family. All too often my husband winds up taking care of *me*, rather than the other way around.

But as I said in the beginning, I never intended to write this from the perspective of one who has arrived. Like you, I am on a journey of small steps, and like you, I sometimes stumble. I look to other examples of motherhood—when the image of the Blessed Virgin looms higher than Mount Everest, I look for something closer to home, such as my sister who has raised two great kids and works full-time (and who, like me, has a genetic pre-disposition to depression). Or my dear friend Elizabeth, who homeschools her four children, and who never seems to raise her voice above a tone best called "mild consternation."

It is here the "endurance" brand of spiritual wait training seems most apt. Looking at the big picture can be overwhelming, so I need to break it into small, repetitive actions. Forego macaroni and cheese in favor of a salad. Walk with the kids to the mailbox down the road, instead of sending them. Watch my favorite TV program—from the treadmill. Backing away from the computer on the dark side of midnight, even though I've caught my second wind and have three deadlines looming ahead of me, so I will have the rest I need to be pleasant to my eager beavers first thing in the morning.

And if one time I choose pasta over rice cakes, I choose better the next day until it becomes second nature. Not because I want to look like a swimsuit model (let's be serious). But because each of these choices help me to "take up my cross" and march a little closer to the perfection God wants to create in me.

When even this small step seems like too much, self-denial requires the partner of humility. There are times when we need other people to help us along the way. For the first three years that we had the kids, God blessed me with a special mentor in this regard. Miss Terri was our pediatrician's nurse and nanny, and she came to see us once or twice a week to lend a hand when I was most desperately in need. More recently, my good friend Katy came to help me put my house in order when I was struggling to maintain my serenity. Now this was not a struggle against gluttony in the sense that I was indulging in high-calorie treats by the bucketful; it was a struggle against flesh nevertheless.

The traditional Lenten disciplines of the Church are best regarded in this light. We do not eat fish sticks on Fridays in order to "earn" a place in heaven; nor do we imagine that by denying ourselves certain luxuries we are somehow more "spiritual" than the rest of the world that goes without them every day. Rather, we do these things to express a desire to put God's will above our own, to discipline our bodies so that the will and reason control the passions, and to acknowledge that the satisfaction of temporal concerns and preferences are of lesser importance than our primary relationship with God and the good of our community.

For Reflection and Discussion

❧ Do you know someone who struggles with depression in ways that have physical manifestations? What might you do to help?

❧ If you were invited to someone's home for dinner on a Friday in Lent, how would you handle it when she brought out her homemade Chicken Parmesan? Is keeping Lent more important than sparing your hostess embarrassment? Why or why not?

❧ Can you think of examples of gluttony (or other abuses of food) that you have encountered? In what ways is this vice "deadly"?

Write your answers to these questions in your Study Guide.

CHAPTER SIX

The Feminine Face of Intimacy

Parent Trap #4: Lust
Virtuous Antidote: Courage

Three things are too wonderful for me;
four I do not understand:
the way of an eagle in the sky,
the way of a serpent on a rock,
the way of a ship on the high seas,
and the way of a man with a maiden.
Proverbs 30:18–19

When I embarked on married life at the age of thirty-five, it was not without a certain amount of relational baggage: I had dated—off and on—for nearly twenty years, and had made my share of mistakes along the way.

Curiously, the two relational mistakes I came to regret most profoundly, and from which it took me the longest to recover, did not involve sex. In each case I had allowed myself to engage in a level of emotional intimacy that (in retrospect) was unwise, given that early on I had realized religious differences prevented us from making a lifelong commitment.

Ironically, in marriage some women make the opposite mistake: Holding their husbands at arms' length emotionally and sometimes even physically. The excuses are many, and often seemingly justified: The desire to avoid pregnancy. The stressful demands of motherhood. Residual guilt from premarital relations (or, less frequently, some inner difficulty in making the adjustment from premarital chastity to marital fidelity). Anxieties surrounding a history of sexual assault or incest—all these things can make it difficult for a woman to give herself 100 percent to her husband. And yet, it is precisely to this level of transparent self-donation to which we have been called.

The Catechism teaches that lust is a "disordered desire for or inordinate enjoyment of sexual pleasure" (2351). Further, it states with regard to married love,

> *Sexuality, by means of which man and woman give*
> *themselves to one another through the acts which are proper*
> *and exclusive to spouses, is not something simply biological,*
> *but concerns the innermost being of the human person as*
> *such. It is realized in a truly human way only if it is an*
> *integral part of the love by which a man and woman commit*
> *themselves totally to one another until death (2361).*

Hearing the word "lust," most of us think in terms of pornography or trashy novels—and some do indeed struggle with such sexual addictions, which can take a lifetime to overcome. Others associate it with promiscuity, particularly related to sexual encounters prior to marriage that leave a distasteful, shameful pall hanging over the marriage bed. Still others equate "lust" with contraception, an intrinsic evil that separates the unitive and procreative aspects of sex.

All these things can contribute to the temerity with which this deadly sin sinks its tentacles into us. However, the root cause is usually a spiritual one: The desire to attain true intimacy solely through physical gratification

God does intend us to achieve a sense of oneness in the sacrament of marriage, the earthly expression of the one eternal Love. And yet, the physical act alone will not suffice unless the soul is also fully engaged.

In the sacrament of marriage, a man and woman is united intimately and inextricably, body and soul. "The two shall be as one flesh," the Bible tells us. In a secondary (and perhaps even "feminine") sense of the word, then, lust involves any choice that distances the spiritual from the physical "oneness" initiated by God through the sacrament of matrimony. Lust isolates the physical and spiritual components of sexual union, seeking the one to the detriment of the other.

For the feminine soul, then, lust may take particular forms: Engaging in physical gratification out of a desire to experience marital intimacy outside of marriage, or because we despair of ever finding our own life's partner. On the other hand, within marriage we must also guard against withholding ourselves spiritually and emotionally, isolating the physical act of sex as an end in itself— whether that end is sought out, or merely endured. Quoting from Pope Paul VI's classic work *Humanae vitae*, Pope John Paul II taught:

> *Like each of the seven sacraments, so also marriage is a real symbol of the event of salvation, but in its own way. "The spouses participate in it as spouses, together, as a couple, so that the first and immediate effect of marriage (res et sacramentum) is not supernatural grace itself, but the Christian conjugal bond, a typically Christian communion of two persons because it represents the mystery of Christ's incarnation and the mystery of His covenant. The content of participation in Christ's life is also specific: conjugal love involves a totality, in which all the elements of the person enter—appeal of the body and instinct, power of feeling and affectivity, aspiration of the spirit and of will. It aims at a deeply personal unity, the unity that, beyond union in one flesh, leads to forming one heart and soul; it demands indissolubility and faithfulness in definitive mutual giving; and it is open to fertility" (cf Humanae vitae, 9).* John Paul II,
> *Familiaris Consortio*, 11, 13

Do You Struggle With Lust?

Therefore, based on the above reading, a "lustful" spirit is one that withholds or withdraws from the fullest and truest expression of marital love, and in so doing ceases to reflect the eternal, divine union of Christ and His Bride, the Church.

In her *Dialogues*, St. Catherine of Siena heard the Lord say, "I can love you more than you can love yourself, and I watch over you a thousand times more carefully than you can watch over yourself."

With that in mind, let's take a look at some of the expressions of this particular deadly sin. Take this little self-test, basing your answers on your most *typical* behavior, based on the preponderance of evidence. Responding positively to several of these questions may indicate you are in need of a "lift" of virtue; consider whether it is strength or endurance that you need.

True or false ...

T/F When my husband does something to annoy or anger me, I withhold sex as punishment.

T/F I sometimes catch myself daydreaming about former loves or potential romantic interests—and I don't always stop myself when I realize what I am doing.

T/F I would be embarrassed if my husband found out some of the romantic daydreams or unwise confidences I have shared with friends. I'm just "letting off steam," but I know it could hurt him.

T/F I believe flirting is harmless and a good confidence booster, so long as it doesn't go any further than just talk.

T/F I've been known to chuckle at the occasional off-color joke at work, to prove I'm not a "prude."

T/F I feel myself tensing up every time my husband touches me a certain way, because I know what is in store, and I'm just not in the mood.

T/F My husband is always the one who initiates sex—and when I "give in," he knows I'm doing him a big favor.

T/F Sometimes I plan the shopping list or engage in other mental "multitasking" during sex.

T/F I routinely fake orgasm, to spare my husband's feelings. Though I love him with all my heart, I find it hard to "let go" and be completely open with him.

T/F There are parts of my past—including but not limited to my sexual past—I have deliberately kept from my husband, my priest, or both.

❧ Action Steps: Defeating Motherly Lust ☙

Do you need endurance or strength in order to overcome this particular weakness in your own life? Consider one or more of the following.

❦ *For endurance:* Is there a particular television program you and your husband watch, but that does not contribute to the health of your marriage? Declare that hour your weekly "date night," and spend that time focusing only on each other. No talking about kids or work or bills. Read a good book aloud to each other, and discuss it. Take a walk under the stars. Plan a dream vacation for after the kids leave home (start putting

loose change in a jar toward that dream, and watch it grow).
Take a bubble bath together. Relax. Enjoy.

☞ *For strength:* Pick up a copy of *Familiaris Consortio* or *Love and Responsibility*, by Pope John Paul II (written before he was pope). Read a few pages each day, and take notes about what you are reading—what insights are particularly meaningful and relevant to your situation? How can you apply them better to family life?

Resilience: The Feminine Face of Courageous Modesty

The caller on "Heart, Mind, and Strength" was understandably perplexed. Her four-year-old daughter would appear several times a day —once even wandering out into the yard—clad in nothing but a pair of tights and a tiara. "Hopefully she'll grow out of it by the time she is sixteen," joked the host, Dr. Gregory Popcak.

Teaching a child to have a proper respect for her body— particularly the "private" areas that are most intimately linked to the vocation of marriage and motherhood—is one of the greatest challenges of parenthood, particularly in our sex-saturated society.

And yet, the virtue of modesty goes far beyond keeping eyes and hands off "forbidden territory." It involves maintaining a delicate balance of the sacred and the ordinary, and of remaining vigilant in clearing away every inordinate sensorial attachment and selfish impulse. Modesty is revealed in every aspect of a woman's manner: how she looks, what she says, and what she does. The Catechism tells us that modesty is a "purity of heart ... which is patience, decency, and discretion. Modesty protects the intimate center of the person" (CCC 2533).

But why does God ask us to preserve this level of decorum? Not because our bodies are ugly or evil, but because of the delicate and sacred purpose for which they were designed. We protect ourselves not because we are weak, but because we were created with an inner strength and vitality that is not only equal to a man's, but in many cases surpasses it. We are, in a word, *resilient*.

Women have been entrusted with a vocation that requires a delicacy of temperament and an intuition that does not rightly belong to men, for they have a different calling. Where men are called to be the "skeleton" of the family, providing for and protecting it, we are the vital "internal organs" of family life, spiritual mothers long before—and in some cases, regardless of whether—we are called to biological motherhood. Modesty, then, is the virtue that seeks to safeguard those capabilities that enable us to fulfill our role steadfastly and well.

With humility we recognize those areas of potential weakness, and admit small failings before they become larger ones. With the feminine gift of intuition, joined with wisdom and discernment, we submit ourselves to the authority and protection of those to whom God has entrusted us. This is not to say we are "helpless," any more than the heart is "helpless" just because it remains in the ribcage. Instead, we are mutually dependent on one another—just as the skeleton is animated only so long as the heart continues to beat.

This is not a popular view in American society, which prizes equality of opportunity and function above all. With the advent of contraception and the ready availability of abortion, many girls are raised to feel as though they are somehow less than a real woman—or, worse, a "prude"—if their sense of modesty prevents them from engaging in all kinds of worldly diversions that offer no lasting benefit. As a result, many have done tremendous damage—body and soul—in an effort to "have it all."

Happily, the enemy need not have the final word. It is never too late to reclaim the graces of virtue and to retrace our steps along the pathway of purity. The damage we do to ourselves (or that others inflict upon us) is real, but the healing graces God has provided are far more powerful than any injury. In this instance, modesty requires not "hiddenness" but transparency, shining the light of truth on our wounds so that the Great Physician may have His way.

If you are struggling with shame and guilt, either over the past or a current shortcoming or trauma, continuing to hide it will only perpetuate the cycle of distance and emotional scarring that prevents true intimacy. Go to a priest or other spiritually mature person you can trust, and let the healing begin today.

For Reflection and Discussion

❧ If a friend came to you and confessed that she no longer loved her husband and was thinking of leaving him, what would you say to her?

❧ If you discovered that your son was experimenting sexually with his long-time girlfriend, what would you do to help the young couple understand the serious consequences of their actions?

❧ Why are frigidity and/or prudishness incompatible with true modesty?

Write your answers to these questions in your Study Guide.

CHAPTER SEVEN

The Feminine Face of Compassion

Parent Trap #5: Anger
Virtuous Antidote: Justice

Good sense makes me slow to anger,
and it is my glory to overlook an offense.
Proverbs 19:11

M y friend recalls meeting her future in-laws for the first time, and noticing that—while their walls were lined with the smiling portraits of their youngest daughter and her family—there was not a single photograph of her sweetheart, Richard. There were many of the younger sister and her husband, who had taken over the family store and turned it into a multi-million dollar business—thanks in no small part to Richard's efforts. He had labored diligently alongside his sister's husband behind the scenes. But Richard's efforts appeared to be largely lost on Jamie's future in-laws.

The situation worsened when, two weeks before the wedding, Jamie's fiancé sheepishly raised the issue of a prenuptial agreement. They were both in their forties, and were marrying for the first time; however, "the family" had decided that, to protect their own interests, Jamie should be made to declare that—regardless of what the future held—she would not make any claims on her future husband's share of the estate.

Trying to keep her voice calm, Jamie took Richard's hands. "My darling, do *you* want this prenup?"

"Oh, I don't know… Since we're never going to divorce anyway, what harm can it do? It will certainly get my family off my back."

"That's true. Divorce is not an option for us. But let's set aside that issue for a moment. Suppose three weeks after our wedding, one of us had a stroke and had to be cared for by the other for the rest of our lives. Would the prenup cover that?"

"No, nothing after the wedding."

"And if tomorrow I went out and won the lottery, would our prenup cover that?"

"That depends on how it was written up…"

A light of inspiration hit. "And if we decided to go on a hot-air balloon ride, and you saw the pilot packing a parachute beforehand, would you wonder about the likelihood of our making it back safely?"

This time her fiancé did not answer right away. Finally, "Yes, I guess I would."

"So why is your family pressuring us to pack a 'marriage parachute'?"

That night, Richard's family was informed there would be no prenup. A week later, the family forced Richard to sell his share of the business. It pained Jamie to see her sweetheart treated so badly, but she was grateful that it gave them a fresh start for their new life together. Richard found another job where he and his gifts were given the appreciation they deserved.

About a year later, Jamie and Richard decided to adopt two children. His parents did not approve—they saw their dreams of a "real" grandchild go up in smoke. Jamie struggled for the first six months of parenthood, but decided not to hold a grudge. Instead, she began dropping in on her mother-in-law, placing the younger child in her lap to coo and smile. Gradually, the thaw became visible as Jamie's mother-in-law realized that, regardless of where the children came from, she was *really* a grandmother.

"It would have been easy to harbor anger toward my husband's family," Jamie admits. "First the money, then the abandonment. There were times when it was all I could do to smile at them across the table at family dinners. But now, when I see my kids run up and hug grandma and grandpa, I know I made the right choice."

Do You Struggle With Anger?

Anger is a desire for revenge (CCC 2302), or an excessive sense of misplaced justice leading one to secure what is "owed" without regard for the good of the other person.

Do you wrestle with this particular deadly sin? Take this little self-test, basing your answers on your most *typical* behavior, based on the preponderance of evidence. Responding positively to several of these questions may indicate you are in need of a "lift" of virtue; consider whether it is strength or endurance that you need.

True or false ...

T/F My mother and/or father used to have such an ugly temper, I was sometimes afraid. I'm even more afraid now that I might turn out just like that.

T/F I frequently say things that I regret the next morning—or even as soon as the words are out of my mouth.

T/F I often have to apologize to coworkers and acquaintances for my angry outbursts.

T/F I am often embarrassed and even alarmed with my own children's outbursts.

T/F I sometimes resort to corporal punishment or other punitive measures with my children simply to vent my own anger.

T/F My children sometimes seem afraid of me, pulling away or running away if they think I'm going to get angry—even if I'm not.

T/F My children tend to ignore my instructions unless I raise my voice or am otherwise harsh with them.

T/F When I get really angry, I lose the ability to think clearly and rationally—doing whatever is necessary to "get even" without regard to long-term consequences.

T/F My husband tracks my hormonal fluxuations out of simple self-preservation, and shields the children from being around me during certain times of the month when my temper flares especially high.

T/F My inability to control my anger has cost me dearly in terms of relationships and other opportunities.

✎ Action Steps: Defeating Motherly Anger ✐

Do you need endurance or strength in order to overcome this particular weakness in your own life? Consider one or more of the following.

❧ *For endurance:* For the next week, take a mental inventory each time you find your temper getting the better of you. What immediately preceded this rush of emotion, and what physical symptoms did you notice? (Face grew hot, fists or jaw clenched, breathing shallowed, head or shoulders tightening, etc.) In retrospect, was it necessary to react this way, or was there a better response? (taking time out, laughing it off, going for a run, breathing deeply). Each time the symptoms arise, imagine yourself blowing out the anger, and breathing in the peace of the Holy Spirit.

⚜ *For strength:* If you lose your temper frequently, it may be a sign that your body is under too much stress, or that there is a physiological cause (such as depression) that needs to be treated by a professional. Make an appointment this week for a complete physical, and talk with your doctor about possible options for you to find the physical and mental release you need. Go to confession ready to talk about the frequency of your outbursts, but also the circumstances that seem to provoke this reaction; your pastor may be able to suggest resources to help you.

"Motherly" Anger—A Lesson in Compassion

My son loves dinosaurs, and particularly enjoys "Dino Planet"— an educational program that depicts through computer-generated imagery how the world's greatest lizards once lived. In one scene, a mother Protoceratops aggressively rushed out to defend her nest against a pack of even more aggressive—and more intelligent— Oviraptors.

Anticipating the mother's angry impulse to rush out to meet the enemy, part of the Oviraptor pack had circled back and attacked the nest from behind. One by one the eggs were dragged from the nest until it was completely empty—a fact the despondent mother discovered only after it was too late.

Seeing the mother dinosaur fly, shrieking and hissing, at the predators reminded me of my own tendency to fly off the handle, particularly when someone close to me is being treated unfairly.

The other day, Craig came home to relate how a frustrated co-worker had made an obscene gesture at him—in front of another employee— shocking Craig into silence in which he marinated for the rest of the day.

That night when Craig came home and told me about what had happened, I was livid. So much so that I began to lambaste my poor sweetheart for not demanding an apology on the spot. Each word from my mouth rubbed salt in his wounded ego, and when I awakened the next morning, it was clear to me that my husband was in a worse state than before. Not only had his co-worker shown complete disregard for his feelings—so had his own wife! Fortunately the situation was resolved—Craig went back to work and discussed with his co-worker how unprofessional his behavior had been, exacting a promise that such a thing would never happen again.

With me, the lesson was learned very differently. Convinced that my reaction to the incident must be due to my own stress level, Craig took a morning off to take the kids swimming, leaving me a couple of hours to work undisturbed. Faced with my anger … he showed me compassion. And his actions reminded me of what I *should* have done, far more effectively than any lecture could have.

Nowhere is the power of the words we use more profound than in our most intimate of relationships—with our husbands and children. The proximity of those dear souls provide ample opportunity to build up the soul both in endurance and strength, if we will take advantage of those unguarded moments in which the monster runs unleashed, that we may conquer it.

For Reflection and Discussion

❦ Talk about the last time you were really angry. What happened —and if you had it to do over again, is there anything you would do differently?

❦ If you saw a mother lose control with her child, what would you do? What suggestions would you give a friend who feels overwhelmed and angry with her children?

❦ Are you ever afraid to show compassion or see things from the other person's point of view simply because you're concerned about the resulting fallout? Talk about it.

Write your answers to these questions in your Study Guide.

CHAPTER EIGHT

The Feminine Face of Hospitality

Parent Trap #6: Greed
Virtuous Antidote: Generosity

Do not be so anxious about a house on earth
when we have such a beautiful one in heaven.
We are poor, but charity compels us.
We must share what God gives among the poor.
St. Soledad

My junior year of high school, I remember my parents struggling to make ends meet as a result of some unexpected medical bills; that year we had hosted an exchange student from Finland, whose parents were coming to visit us for a month at Easter. The prospect of needing to feed *three* extra mouths forced my parents to stretch their faith even more than they already had.

One night after they had attempted—futilely—to balance the checkbook, my parents had a whispered conversation about whether to have Jaana placed with another family. They had no idea how we were going to feed her, let alone her parents, for another month. I held my breath as I lay in bed that night, listening to their discussion. I understood that times were tough—for all her ingenuity, mom could stretch the soup only so far. Still, I hoped for a miracle.

The next morning I was awakened to the sound of pounding downstairs—my bedroom window was above the front door. I ran downstairs and found my father and Jaana coming in from outside, laughing good-naturedly. "What's going on?" I asked.

"Your father put up a welcome sign for my parents," giggled Jaana. Sure enough, under the mailbox was a Popsicle stick with blue letters. I bent down to examine the stick, but could not quite make out what it said.

"Tervetuloa," Jaana told me. "It means 'welcome' in Finnish."

I was so lighthearted, I fairly hummed as I set the breakfast table. Jaana was going to stay, after all.

Over pancakes that morning, Dad prayed, "Lord, today we need Your help in taking care of our guests. Our friends at church have already done so much, and it's not fair to ask them to do any more. Right now, we're asking You to provide what we need."

Later that morning, as we piled into the car to go to church, Dad reminded us again. "I mean it. Not a word to anyone. Let's just trust God." I wondered about this all the way to church. How was God going to help us, if not through our church family?

I didn't have long to wonder. That afternoon as we returned from church, the front porch door was propped open. "That's strange," Dad said. "You all stay here. I'm going to see what's going on."

The next thing we heard was the big, booming sound of my father's laugh. "Come here, Sandy, you've got to see this." That was enough to bring the rest of us running as well.

On that porch, large as life, were ten huge boxes of groceries. Hams and bread and cheese and vegetables—all still cold, as if someone had just left them there. Enough food for a year, I thought! Best of all, on top of the biggest box was a triple-layer devil's food cake with fudge frosting. As my mother went from box to box, exclaiming over each new find, I dedicated myself to guarding the cake plate, swiping the occasional surreptitious dab of frosting.

We never did find out who left the groceries—though the

fudge frosting tasted just like the kind Mom's friend Nancy made. However, Nancy seemed as surprised and pleased as everyone else when we gave thanks at church that evening. As for me, I assumed God had a Finnish "chocolate cake" angel who flew by, saw the Popsicle "Tervetuola," and figured the welcome was just for her.

Now that I'm older and (hopefully) a bit wiser, I realize that something else was at work here.

Some might argue that simple prudence might have induced my parents to have our exchange student placed in another home. Our resources were limited, and their primary responsibility was to their own children. Instead, they exercised their faith muscles. As a result, their family was fed with abundance—and their children learned an important, practical lesson on trusting in God's providence.

Do You Struggle with Greed?

Take this little self-test, basing your answers on your most typical behavior, based on the preponderance of evidence (or how you think the person closest to you would answer on your behalf). Responding positively to several of these questions may indicate you are in need of a "lift" of virtue; consider whether it is strength or endurance that you need.

True or false …

T/F I hold on to outgrown clothes and unused household items, even if I don't have an immediate need for them. I might need them someday.

T/F When donating canned goods to the local food bank, I search my pantry shelves for stuff that I know I'll never use, rather than what I know they need.

T/F I believe people are basically selfish, and that if I don't actively protect my family, someone will take advantage of them.

T/F I would never drive a second-hand car, or force my kids to wear second-hand clothes, or brown-bag lunches. We make good money, so there is no need!

T/F We regularly spend more than we earn—mostly by maxing out credit cards.

T/F I find it hard to get along with my in-laws because they always seem to give more support to their other kids than to our family —even though we need it more.

T/F When I come out of a general merchandise store (like K-Mart) I always wind up spending more than I'd planned.

T/F I haunt garage and yard sales—even though we don't really need anything, there's always something I just HAVE to have.

T/F I hang up on charity solicitors and dump their appeal letters in the trash—if you give once, they'll hound you for life!

T/F If God determined the size of our "heavenly home" by multiplying our earthly donations by ten (since the "tithe" means "tenth"), we would not have enough celestial currency for a mud hut.

✣ Action Steps: Defeating Motherly Greed ✢

Do you need endurance or strength in order to overcome this particular weakness in your own life? Consider one or more of the following.

❦ *For endurance:* Pick up a copy of Dale O'Leary's *Too Much Stuff!* and spend one day in each area of your home sorting through your possessions to determine what you no longer need, and what someone else could put to better use. Each day for one month, dispose of at least one thing either by donation or by throwing it away. If there is a particular area where you struggle with over-accumulation (for me, it's books), resolve not to acquire any more unless you get rid of an equal number you already own.

❦ *For strength:* The principle of the "tithe"—giving one-tenth of all you possess to God and His Church—is one that many Christians have experienced great blessing by following. Consider your contribution last year; what can you do to bring that figure closer to the 10% mark, either in outright financial contribution or in time, or a combination of both?

Hospitality: The Feminine Face of Generosity

Order and proportion, beauty and moderation: To embrace these principles of artistry within the home is to create an environment where the senses of family members are liberated to appreciate the fullness of God's design. A single bite of sun-ripened peach dances on the tongue with a far greater satisfaction—and far less guilt—than a quart of factory processed frozen yogurt.

True hospitality—the ability to tend to another person's needs while simultaneously putting that person at ease—demands both an empathetic perspective and an artistic touch. The generous person slips a check in a get-well card; the hospitable individual also leaves a jar of homemade chicken-and-dumplings or an inspirational book on tape.

But what does practicing the art of hospitality have to do with combating greed, one might ask? Just as the greed attaches to material things out of fear or pride, the one who practices true hospitality meets the physical needs of others out of an inner conviction of faith and trust, demonstrating by their own detachment a firm reliance on the only true Source of good things.

The motivation behind the act is as important as the act itself. Some people, for example, give not out of a sense of gratitude, but out of neediness—a need to be liked, or to be in the limelight. As a child, I remember going to the home of my mother's friend, whom we called "Aunt Nan." She was a buxom Italian "career woman" (back when most women I knew were wives and mothers) who took in stray cats and homeless children with great passion and enthusiasm, even if they didn't always return her effusive affections. If there was a new family in church, they were always invited over to dinner that afternoon for her justifiably famous Chicken Parmesan, and if there wasn't a new family, we were usually the lucky recipients of her culinary efforts.

That's not to say she was perfect. Years after I had left home, I heard through the grapevine that Aunt Nan had been indicted for embezzlement, and she wound up serving prison time. She confessed to her crime—it seems her generosity got a little out of hand when she started "borrowing" increasingly large sums from her employer, always intending to pay him back, to pay for lavish gifts for friends and family.

In her inordinate desire to be loved and admired, she lost a piece of herself. Ironically, she received the affirmation she wanted along with her sentence: Despite the financial devastation she had brought upon him, her husband stuck by his wife through it all. So did their church community, as those who had been recipients of Nancy's kindness kept him in casseroles for the duration of her incarceration.

Hospitality, the "sister companion" of generosity, has a relational component that cannot be separated from the virtue itself. While people can be generous for many reasons—including wanting to "play" benefactor (in terms as grand as possible, despite the possible damage it might do to the dignity of the recipient)—the truly empathetic always show kindness with the welfare of the recipient in mind.

How does this relate to greed? We have explored each vice in relation to its corresponding virtue, the idea being that a particular sin is deadly for the simple reason that it is contrary to the good—that is, the immediate good of the community (physical good) and the ultimate spiritual good, which is unbroken communion with God.

When we practice empathetic generosity, this relational component that is damaged by greed is restored: By ministering to the physical needs of those around us, we strengthen the bonds of community and acknowledge our own dependence on Divine Providence.

For Reflection and Discussion

❧ Take another look at the final question in the greed "self-test." If God multiplied your generosity by ten, what do you think your celestial home would look like?

❧ "God helps those who help themselves" is a favorite American truism—but it is found nowhere in Scripture. Is the sentiment itself "Christian"? Why or why not?

❧ Have there been situations in your life when you have found it difficult to trust God, in which you felt obligated to "fix" or supply for yourself? In retrospect, is there anything you would do differently?

Write your answers to these questions in your Study Guide.

CHAPTER NINE

The Feminine Face of Industry

Parent Trap #7: Sloth
Virtuous Antidote: Prudence

A good wife, who can find? She is far more precious than jewels. The heart of her husband trusts in her, and he will have no lack of gain. She does him good, and not harm, all the days of her life. ...

She rises while it is yet night and provides food for her household and tasks for her maidens. She considers a field and buys it; with the fruit of her hands she plants a vineyard. She girds her loins with strength and makes her arms strong. ...Her lamp does not go out at night. ...

She opens her hand to the poor, and reaches out her hands to the needy. She is not afraid of snow for her household, for all her household are clothed in scarlet. She makes herself coverings; her clothing is fine linen and purple.

Her husband is known in the gates, when he sits among the elders of the land. ... Strength and dignity are her clothing, and she laughs at the time to come. She opens her mouth with wisdom, and the teaching of kindness is on her tongue. She looks well to the ways of her household, and does not eat the bread of idleness. Her children rise up and call her blessed; her husband also, and he praises her: "Many women have done excellently, but you surpass them all."

Proverbs 31:10–29

I can always tell when I'm spending too much time in front of my computer: our border collie leaves a hairy trail across the living room, the dining room table gets buried, and Christopher can't find his socks in the morning. When it gets really bad, a built-in radar just under my epidermis starts giving off little tingly alarms, and my scalp gets tight. Finally, I have enough, and start tossing things around like a woman possessed.

"Look out!" Craig calls out. "Mommy's on the warpath!" To my eternal gratitude, he grabs the kids and the dog and runs for the park, confident that when he returns in four hours, it will be to a cleaner house and a calmer wife. Well, calmer at least until the next time he leaves his shoes in the middle of the floor....

As mothers, we sometimes find it difficult to relate to this paragon of virtue, the Queen of Proverbs 31. We get caught up in the inconvenience. The frustration. The clamoring for five minutes of peace and quiet. And then Sloth makes its appearance: "This is too much. There must be an easier way. Surely God doesn't expect you to kill yourself for these ungrateful urchins!"

No, of course not. But He does expect us to die a little every day, all for love of Him. Little by little, we build up our stamina: Each time we get out of bed to chase away a bad dream, or set aside our work for the umpteenth game of "Candyland," or give the forty bajillionth lesson in table etiquette ("No, Christopher, you may *not* use the same hand you just used to wipe your nose to grab another hotdog from the plate. Tongs are much better.")

And if this were the outside limits of "sloth," even that would be bearable. However, God does not want us only to work on perfecting our children—He wants us to zero in on our own behavior as well. "Yes, My dear child. I know you've been putting off matching that carload of unmatched socks in the dining room buffet. Hop to it—and while you're at it, why not turn off the sitcom and put on that Gospel tape series you got for Christmas?"

Do You Struggle With Sloth?

The *Baltimore Catechism* (Q311) teaches that "sloth is a laziness of the mind and body, through which we neglect our duties on account of the labor they require." This encourages us to set aside our spiritual responsibilities, especially cultivating a deeper prayer life.

Do you wrestle with this particular deadly sin? Take this little self-test, basing your answers on your most *typical* behavior, based on the preponderance of evidence (or how you think the person closest to you would answer on your behalf). Responding positively to several of these questions may indicate you are in need of a "lift" of virtue; consider whether it is strength or endurance that you need.

True or false ...

T/F When I have a free moment, I am far more likely to turn on the TV than pick up a Bible or other good book. If I had to put my hand on a Bible right now, I wouldn't know where to find one.

T/F At least six mornings out of seven, my children beat me out of bed (sometimes literally).

T/F I have difficulty establishing and maintaining a regular prayer time—even a five-minute quiet time while driving carpool.

T/F My children pester me constantly for attention simply because I have not established a set daily routine, so they know what to expect.

T/F Although my children are old enough to do chores, I find it easier simply to do the work myself. My six-year-old thinks the iron is a "dragon tooth," and my daughter believes in the "dishwasher fairy" who unloads the dishes while she sleeps.

T/F My family could not possibly survive without electricity for a day —the kids wouldn't know what to do with themselves without a TV! (I'm not sure I would, either.)

T/F My "garden" has a weed-to-flower (or plant) ratio of about 13:1.

T/F I have not cleaned out the refrigerator or vacuumed under the furniture since the **first** Bush administration.

T/F If I had to cook everything from scratch for a week, my kids could subsist on peanut butter and jelly—if I could dig out my bread maker.

T/F I have not walked more than a mile anywhere – except maybe in the mall – since I became a mother. It's easier just to hop in the car, so I know we have everything we need at all times.

✒ Action Steps: Defeating Motherly Sloth ✒

Do you need endurance or strength in order to overcome this particular weakness in your own life? Consider one or more of the following.

☙ *For endurance:* Take a personal inventory and determine whether there are physical reasons for your lack of energy. Are you getting enough sleep? Are you eating properly and getting enough exercise? Do you have a set daily schedule, or just do what you feel like it, when you feel like it?

Establishing these personal disciplines are an important part of getting yourself back on track. Create a personal mission statement, and list five "daily disciplines" (such as eating at least three servings of fruit and vegetables, and drinking five glasses of water each day). Some days the "Sloth Monster" may get the better of you; that's OK, just breathe a quick prayer for grace and start fresh the next day!

☙ *For strength:* Is there a large task you've been needing to do, but are finding it hard to get motivated? Consider partnering with a "Task Buddy," promising to return the favor in exchange for her physical help and/or babysitting services. Once the job is done, treat yourselves to a small but personally meaningful reward!

Finally, A great man of God once observed, "I have so much to do today that I must first devote an extra hour to prayer." Do you have a regular prayer time? If not, commit to getting up an extra fifteen minutes early. Also consider turning off the TV earlier each evening, to give you time to get ready for the next day and to spend a few moments of quality time with your beloved—your husband, and your God.

Industry: The Feminine Face of *Prudence*

Even with my flu-infested brain, the crash was loud enough to send me springing from my bed. Bleary-eyed and shuffling, I emerged from the bedroom to find my children had taken my dear husband hostage, Cheerios scattered like little land minds around his feet. By the looks of things, he had spent all morning trying to unload the dishwasher with one hand, type on his computer with the other, and talk on his cell phone with a … third?

I don't know about yours, but my husband definitely did not come with the multitasking gene.

As I moved through the room, simultaneously directing the kids to get the dustpan, sweeping last night's pizza crusts into the trash, and setting out crayons and workbooks for a little "table time," there was an unmistakable light of respect ablaze in Craig's hazel eyes. "How do you *do* that?" he breathed with wonder.

Truth be told, even *with* the multitasking gene I struggle to keep things together. Piles of laundry mount up in the hamper and on the couch (clearly everyone but me still believes in the "Laundry Fairy" who takes clothes warm from the dryer, folds them, and returns them to their drawers complete with matched socks). And not only does a quarter *not* bounce off my hospital corners, it usually gets lost in the pile of shirts waiting to be put away in my husband's closet.

Maybe it's just the rose-colored glasses of childhood at work, but I don't remember my mother's house ever looking like mine. She fed a family of five on a shoestring—sometimes as little as $50 a week. She sewed and canned and made piecrust from scratch. Her house was always company-ready, and she usually had a casserole in the freezer that she could whip out in emergencies. She was at the church, usually running some program, every time the doors opened. And she taught us all the fine art of homemaking from the time we were old enough to hold a broom.

It seems I should be in the Proverbs 31 remedial class. How did she do it all? In his book, *Guiltless Catholic Parenting,* Bert Ghezzi gave me a tool to help me sort out the difference between busyness (juggling twelve balls just because I can) and true industry (working diligently to accomplish the goals that are most essential to my vocation). Not surprisingly, the method requires a liberal dash of the "Sloth Monster antidote"—prudence.

Draw a box, then cross two lines so you have four little boxes inside (see diagram). Label the vertical axis "important" and "unimportant" (that is, things that are more essential or less essential to your primary vocation) and the horizontal one "urgent" and "not urgent." Then you start placing your "to do" list on the grid, asking God to help you decide the priority for each.[1]

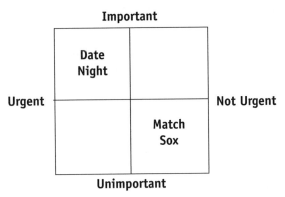

"Date night" with your sweetheart? You know it's important—and only you can tell when it becomes urgent, when you're starting to lose touch. Similarly, spending time with the kids is "important." But what is most urgent—their science project (due next week), teaching them to wash windows, or playing Candyland? You decide. Then focus most of your efforts each day on the important/urgent quadrant, and move on from there.

While you are prioritizing, take a look at the state of your "spiritual house" as well as the physical one. Has your "Mommy Monster" been getting the better of you lately? Have you been neglecting yourself in ways that are eroding into the health and happiness of your family? Is there a personal shortcoming that you know you need to fix, but have not found the time or energy to devote to it? Starting today, work it into your plan. In the words of Amy Carmichael:

[1] The assignations may change from week to week—when your husband runs out of clean socks in his drawer, for example, matching socks may move from the "unimportant/not urgent" to "unimportant/urgent" or even "important/urgent."

"Blessed are the single-hearted, for they shall enjoy much peace. If you refuse to be hurried and pressed, if you stay your soul on God, nothing can keep you from that clearness of spirit that is life and peace. In that stillness you will know what His will is."

For Reflection and Discussion

❧ What personal limitations do you sometimes find yourself using as an excuse to take the "easy way," and do you think you need to take steps to change this?

❧ What household or personal chore (such as going to the dentist) have you been putting off that you will tackle this week?

❧ Is there a certain habit of your mother's—washing the floors by hand, for example, or refusing to use a cake mix—that you have integrated into your own life simply because you feel guilty about doing it any other way? This week ask God for an extra measure of prudence, to help you decide whether it is time to find a "new and improved" way to accomplish the same task!

Write your answers to these questions in your Study Guide.

CHAPTER TEN

Raising Up Mommy: A "Pick-Me-Up" Plan

The Lord shows exceeding great mercy to him whom
He gives grace and courage to resolve to strive after this
blessing with all his might. For God denies Himself to no one
who perseveres, but gradually increases the courage
of such a one till he achieves victory.
Autobiography of
Teresa of Avila (Chap.XI)

And if any one loves righteousness, her labors are virtues;
for she teaches self-control and prudence, justice and
courage; nothing in life is more profitable ... than these.
Wisdom of Solomon 8:7

Though she entered the convent to escape the demands of home and hearth, this sixteenth-century Spanish noblewoman became the spiritual mother of generations of Carmelites who wanted to follow God with a singularity of spirit. To guide them, she penned two of the most revered spiritual volumes of all time: *The Way of Perfection* and *The Interior Castle*. It is this first work that we will touch upon in this chapter.

In chapter four, St. Teresa of Avila writes: "...it is very important that we understand how much the practice of these three things helps us to possess inwardly and outwardly the peace our Lord recommended so highly to us. The first of these is love for one another; the second is detachment from all created things; the third is true humility, which, even though I speak of it last, is the main practice and embraces all the others." [2]

[2] Kavanaugh, *The Collected Works of Teresa of Avila*, Vol. 2 (Washington, D.C.: ICS, 1980), 54.

Although she was writing primarily to her sisters when she penned these words, St. Teresa's observation provides rich food for thought for us as well. Through the lens of family, we learn to love more perfectly, letting go of all that is not of eternal importance in order to cling to that which is.

In previous chapters, we have explored each of the serious vices and considered how they might be manifesting themselves in our lives. Understanding that the cultivation of virtue (and detachment from vice) is a gradual process, it may be helpful for you to consider each of them in turn—with which of these do you struggle most? Which do you think God wants you to tackle, by the grace of the Spirit, with the greatest vehemence?

In the chart below, place an "x" on the spectrum of vice and virtue, to indicate where you think you are today. Then mark the two or three of which you feel most in need of personal growth.

PRIDE	HUMILITY
ENVY	TRUST
GLUTTONY	TEMPERANCE
LUST	MODESTY
ANGER	JUSTICE
GREED	GENEROSITY
SLOTH	PRUDENCE

The "Feelings" Trap

Let's face it: We are passionate creatures. While men tend to focus on the facts at hand, women often rely on less objective (and what often turn out to be an equally important) factors. Intuition and "sense" factor heavily into the decisions we make every day. As wives and mothers, we tend to "go with our gut." That is how God designed us to be.

There are times, of course, when our feelings and emotions trip us up. Hormones may factor in to it, but just as often there are other considerations: Anxiety over a challenge facing a family member, frustration over a particular set of circumstances over which we have little or no control, and unresolved relational issues top the list.

The *Catechism* tells us that these feelings are not sinful—unless we use them as an excuse not to do what we know is right (or do what we know is wrong).

> *Strong feelings are not decisive for the morality or the holiness of persons; they are simply the inexhaustible reservoir of images and affections in which the moral life is expressed. Passions[3] are morally good when they contribute to a good action, evil in the opposite case. The upright will orders the movements of the senses it appropriates to the good and to beatitude; an evil will succumbs to disordered passions and exacerbates them. Emotions and feelings can be taken up into the virtues or perverted by the vices* (CCC#1768).

Returning to the illustration of the weight trainer, a woman can choose to "push past the pain" in order to take her stamina to the next level—or when her energy level is low, she can give in to the little voice inside that whispers, "Oh, let's just skip it today. Remember that pint of Haagen-Dazs you squirreled away in the back of the freezer?"

Similarly, when our "Mommy Monster" kicks in, there is a point of decision.

---

[3] The principal passions are love and hatred, desire and fear, joy, sadness, and anger. (CCC 1772).

❦ Am I going to yell at my child for embarrassing me, or am I going to take him aside and patiently remind him of what is expected?

❦ Am I going to nag my husband about taking out the trash (again), or choose to see the overflowing can as an opportunity to demonstrate my love for him and trust that God will work in my husband by my quiet example?

❦ Am I going to indulge in that Haagen Dazs, or grab a bottle of water and invite the kids to go on a nature walk?

❦ Am I going to go about my own routine every night, or am I going to go into my husband's study and give him a backrub and ask him about his day?

❦ Am I going to hold on to that grudge against my mother-in-law until she apologizes, or am I going to look for a way to show kindness to her?

❦ Am I going to get vengeance with a credit card the next time I'm feeling neglected, or am I going to look for a way to share what I have with someone who needs it more?

❦ Am I going to dedicate a week to de-cluttering my house, or simply think up some creative excuses the next time unexpected company drops in?

✎ Action Step:
Cultivating 3 Weapons Every Woman Warrior Needs ✐

❦ **Prayer.** When we are feeling strong, it's important to "store up" the graces we will need in the hard times ahead. When we are feeling weak, we need "reinforcements"—not only those close to us here on earth, but the saints who intercede for us in heaven. Allow the Holy Trinity to encircle you, and call upon the Blessed Mother and your guardian angel to stand guard during your "down" times.

❦ **Sacraments.** Those who are in training need to eat properly. Receive the Eucharist and spend time with the Blessed Sacrament as often as you can. Keep short accounts with God by making a daily examination of conscience, and go to confession frequently—weekly, if you can manage it.

❦ **Choose Virtue.** When a particular vice is rearing its ugly head, it isn't enough to say "No" to the sin—we must also say "Yes!" to its corresponding virtue. When the evil one sees that the temptation is not only failing, but causing him to lose ground, he will resort to it less and less often. Above all, remember to acknowledge to those you have injured—particularly your children—when you fall short.

Tapping Into the Weapons of the Spirit

*Therefore take the whole armor of God, so that you may be able to withstand in the evil day, and having done all, to stand. Stand therefore, having **girded your loins with truth**, and having put on the **breastplate of righteousness**, and having shod your feet with the **equipment of the gospel of peace**; besides all these, taking the **shield of faith**, with which you can quench all the flaming darts of the evil one. And take*

the **helmet of salvation**, and the **sword of the Spirit**, which
is the word of God.

Pray at all times in the Spirit, with all prayer and
supplication. To that end keep alert with all perseverance,
making supplication for all the saints, and also for me, that
utterance may be given me in opening my mouth boldly to
proclaim the mystery of the gospel ...

Ephesians 6:13–19

Through the sanctifying grace of baptism (CCC#1266), we
have been given every spiritual resource we need in order to
slay "Mommy Monster"!

When the evil one conspires to lure us into a "pity pit" as a
toddler clutches our thighs, refusing to detach, we can listen to
the whisper of the Spirit. "Child of Mine, I love you. Draw
close to Me—even closer than your child is to you right now.
Know that I long to hear you even more than your child wants
you to hear *her*."

When a family member makes a choice that breaks our
heart, God's grace enables us to choose holiness over self-
righteousness. "How often, My dear daughter, have you made
choices that cost Me even more than this choice is costing you?
Put on your breastplate, dear one, that the darts of bitterness
and resentment will never find their mark. I will carry you
through this, too."

When we are faced with a situation in which there seems to
be no good choice, and in despair we are tempted to say or do
something that would cause even greater injury, our "shoes of
peace" will keep us on the right path. "You are beautiful, My
dear daughter, inside and out. Step aside, and let My light shine
through you."

When those we love are stumbling in the dark, the "shield of
faith" serves a dual purpose: So long as we stick together, some

may use their shields for covering—and others, for carrying those who have fallen. "Take up your shield, my daughter. If you lay it down, even when no battle seems eminent, you may find yourself like the foolish virgins (see Mt 25:1ff), unprepared when the time comes."

When doubts assail us, wondering whether God could truly love "a wretch like me," our helmet of salvation will cover presumption and condemnation alike. "My grace is sufficient for you, My daughter. There is nothing you have done, nothing you could do, that will take you out of reach of My Mercy. Put on your helmet, and feel your loving Father's hand upon your head—and know that, even when the battle is the bloodiest, you are worth every drop to Me."

And finally, when the rancid breath of the enemy makes our hair stand on end — when every message we hear gives us cause to become angry or embittered—remember that God has provided His Word as a place of refuge and hope. In the Scriptures He feeds our minds, transforming them into beacons of truth; in the Eucharist—the Word made flesh—He restores our souls. "Take up your sword, My child. Trust me, it is not too heavy for you to bear. My very life is within you, giving you all the strength you will ever need."

For Reflection and Discussion

❦ Do you find that certain temptations are especially strong during certain times—perhaps even connected with your menstrual cycle? Keeping a spiritual diary may help you to see the "vice prints" more clearly, and help you to recognize a trap before you fall in.

❦ Have you ever considered going to a spiritual director? Someone who can sit with you and talk about your progress—both the challenges, and the areas where you would like to grow? Consider talking with your pastor about finding a good one.

❦ Write a letter to God. Tell Him about the vices you find most shameful, and ask Him to help you ... starting today ... to turn around and begin pursuing the corresponding virtue. Take the letter with you to the Sacrament of Reconciliation, and read it aloud. Let the healing begin today!

Write your answers to these questions in your Study Guide.

About the Author:

Heidi Saxton and her husband Craig are adoptive parents of two children. She is available for speaking engagements. You may reach her through the publisher, or contact her directly at hsaxton@christianword.com. You may also read more of her work online at CatholicMom.com and CatholicExchange.com. She has three blogs that she updates frequently:

*Mommy Monsters (mommymonsters.blogspot.com) for perpetually challenged parents.

*Silent Canticle (heidihesssaxton.blogspot.com) for writers, especially those who would like to write for "Canticle" magazine.

*Streams of Mercy (streamsofmercy.blogspot.com) for those who want to grow in faith.